I0485278

# An Artful Adventure

## Hidden Picture Coloring For Everyone!

---

## By Jennie Mathis Nelson

### Copyright © 2015

All rights reserved.  This is a work of fiction and art.  All images in this book are original illustrations by Jennie Mathis Nelson.  Names, characters, places, and incidents either are the product of the author's imagination or are used fictitiously.  Any resemblance to actual persons, living or dead, events, or locales is entirely coincidental.

No part of this book may be reproduced or transmitted in any form or by any means, electronic or mechanical, including photo copying, recording or by any information storage and retrieval system without the written permission of the author, except for quotes used in book reviews.

Welcome to a fun and Artful Adventure!  This is where you are truly allowed to be yourself and express yourself any way you want.  There are no rules here!  Beyond the pages of coloring, a hidden adventure also awaits your exploration.  Through each page, you can enter the world that best suits how you feel or how you'd *like* to feel, and because we feel different every day, the scenes each have their own personality.  Some are more adventurous, some are edgy with rock stars and dinosaurs, and a few are happily whimsical.

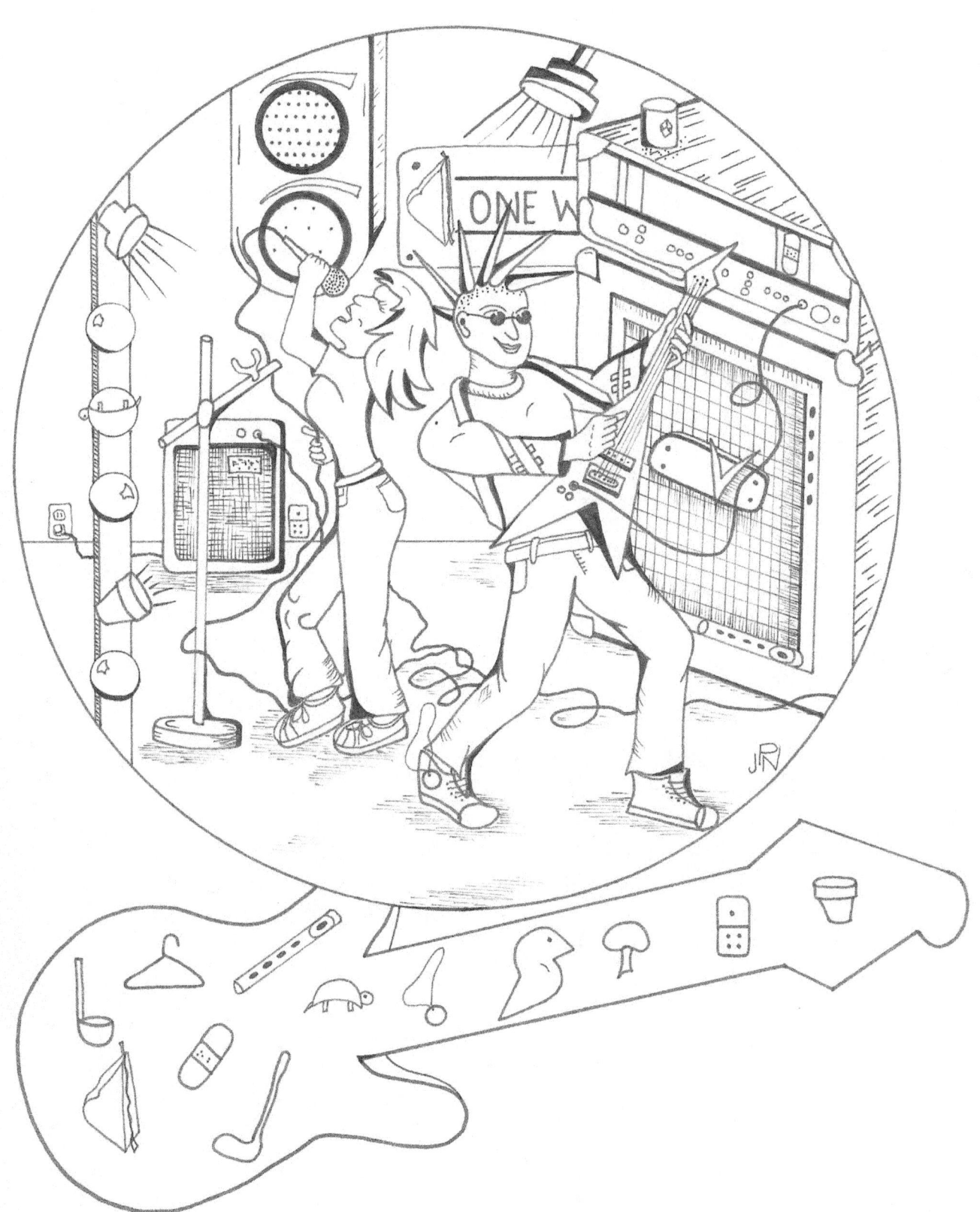

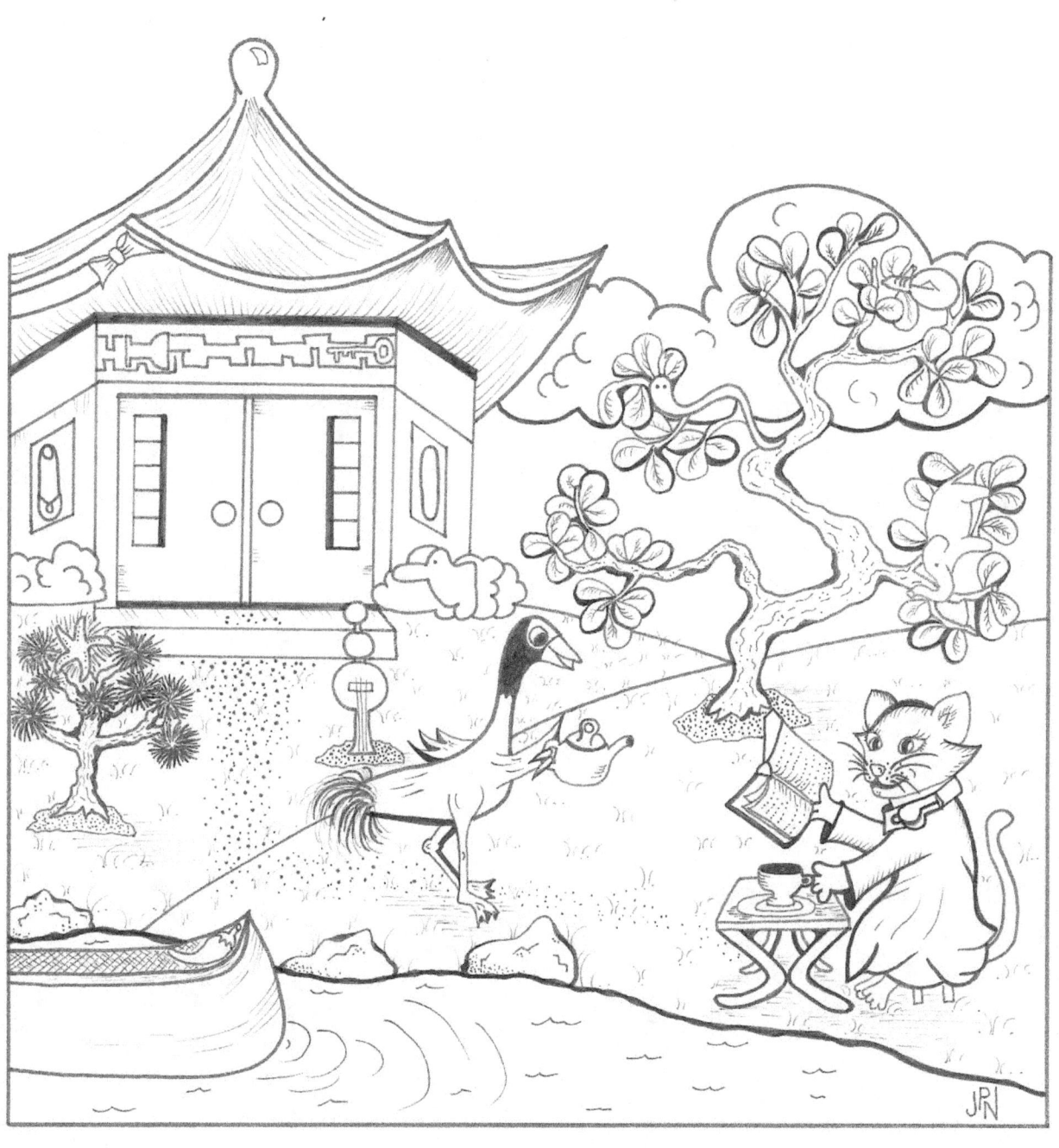

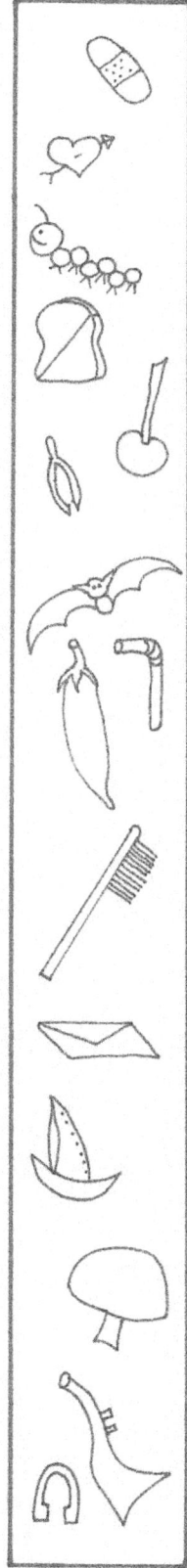

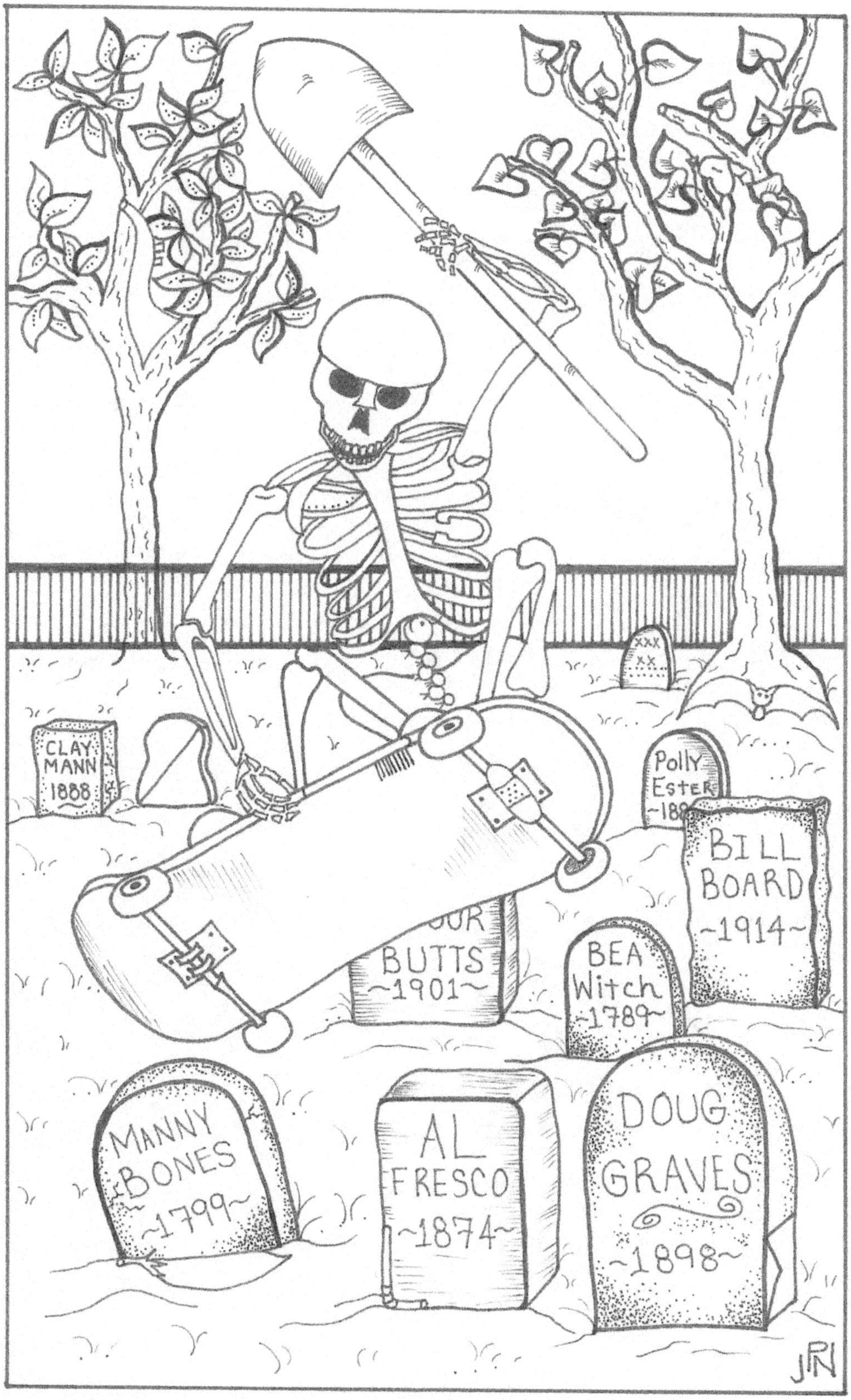

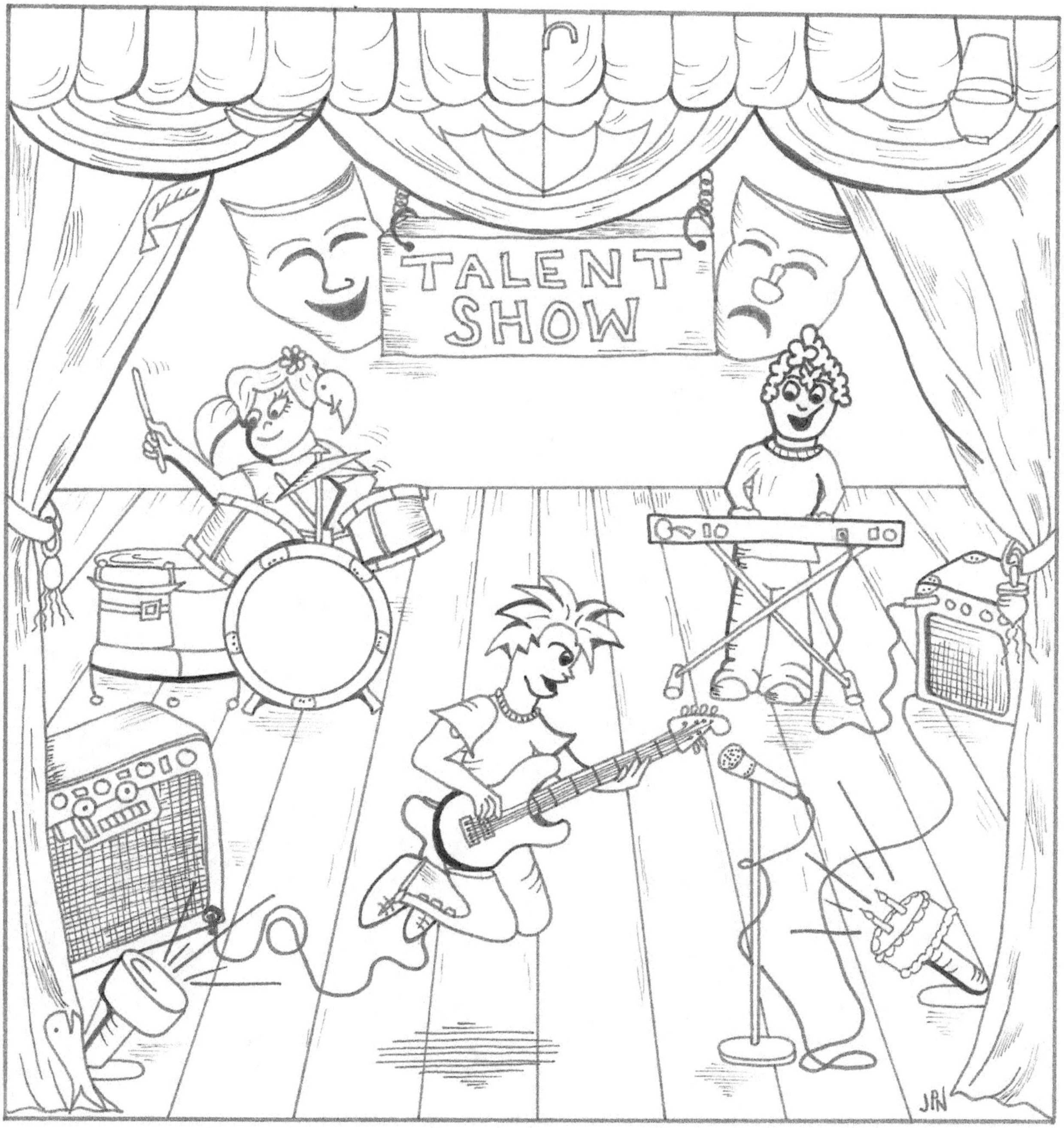

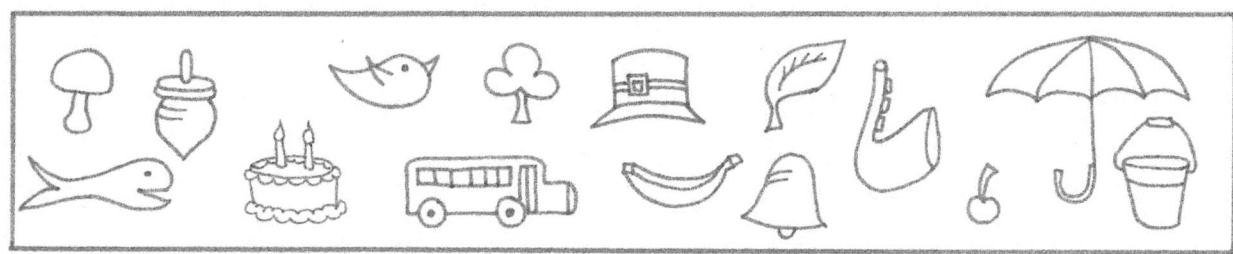

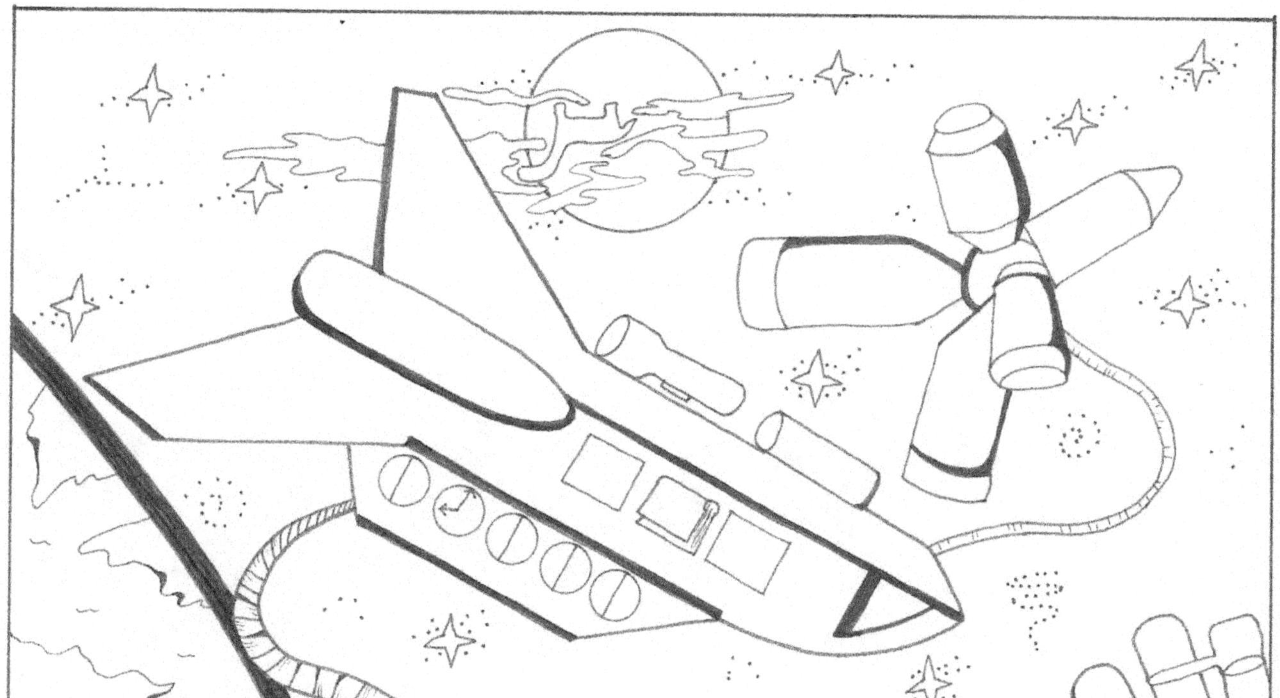

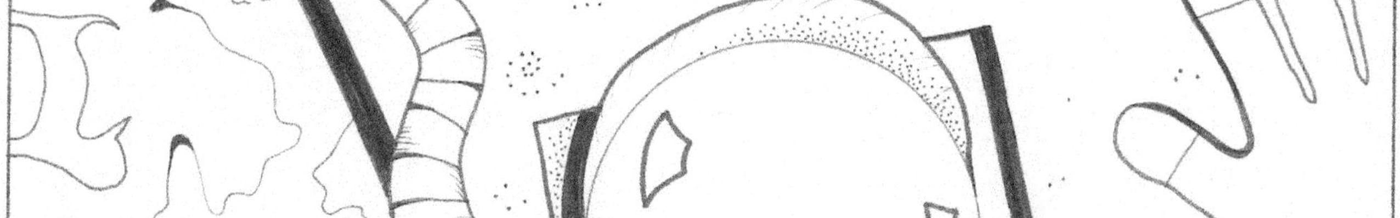

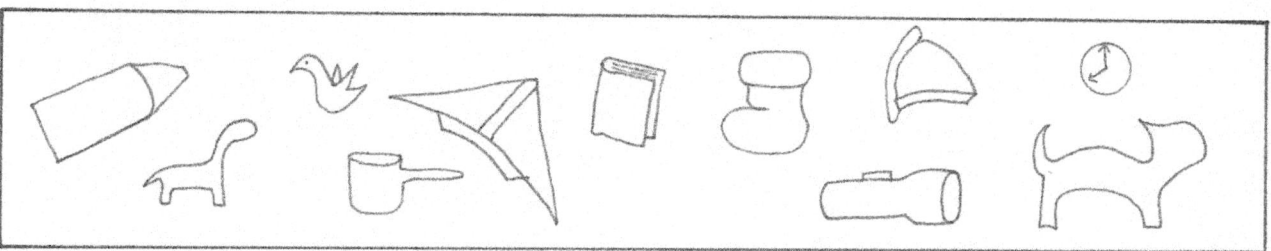

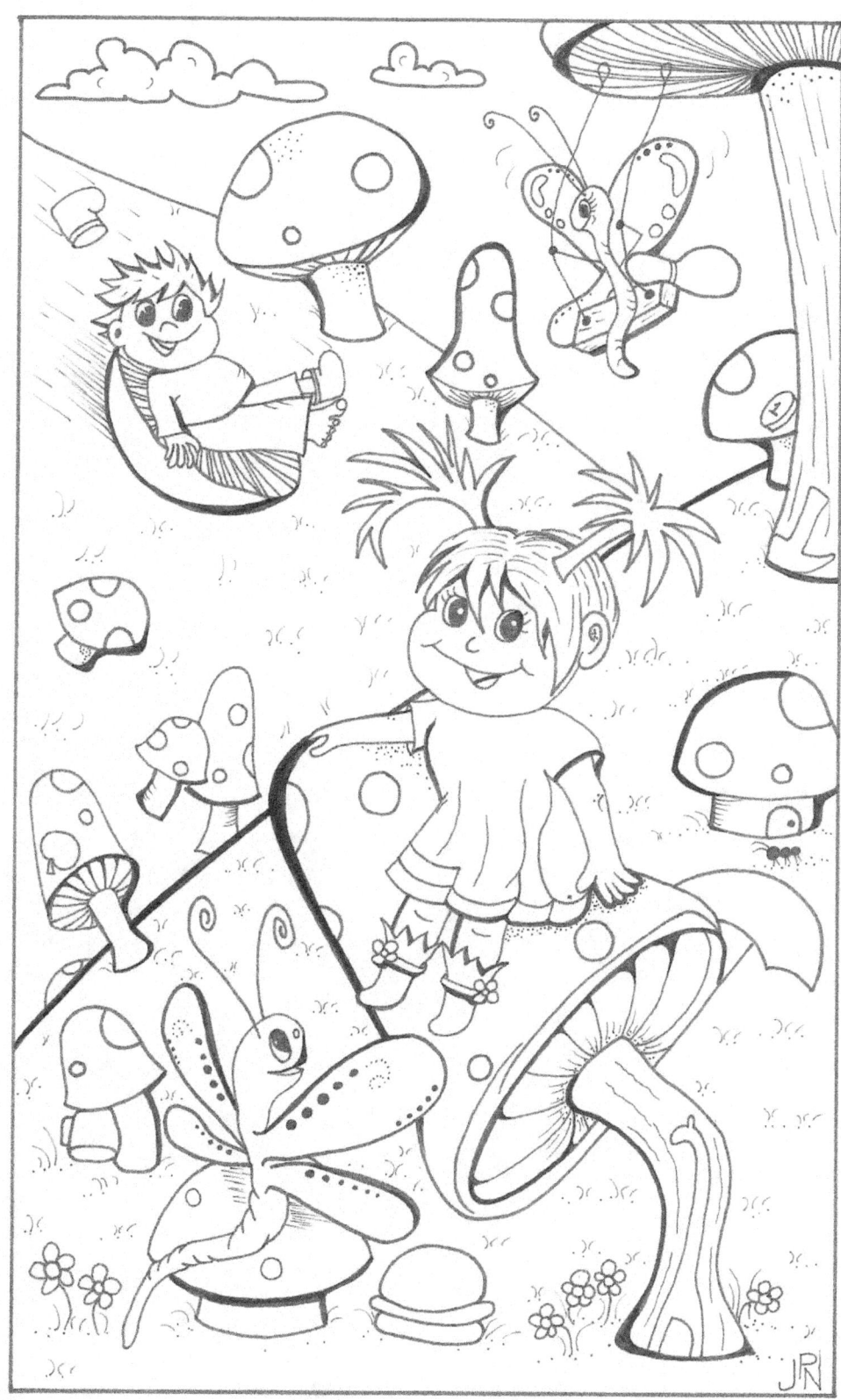

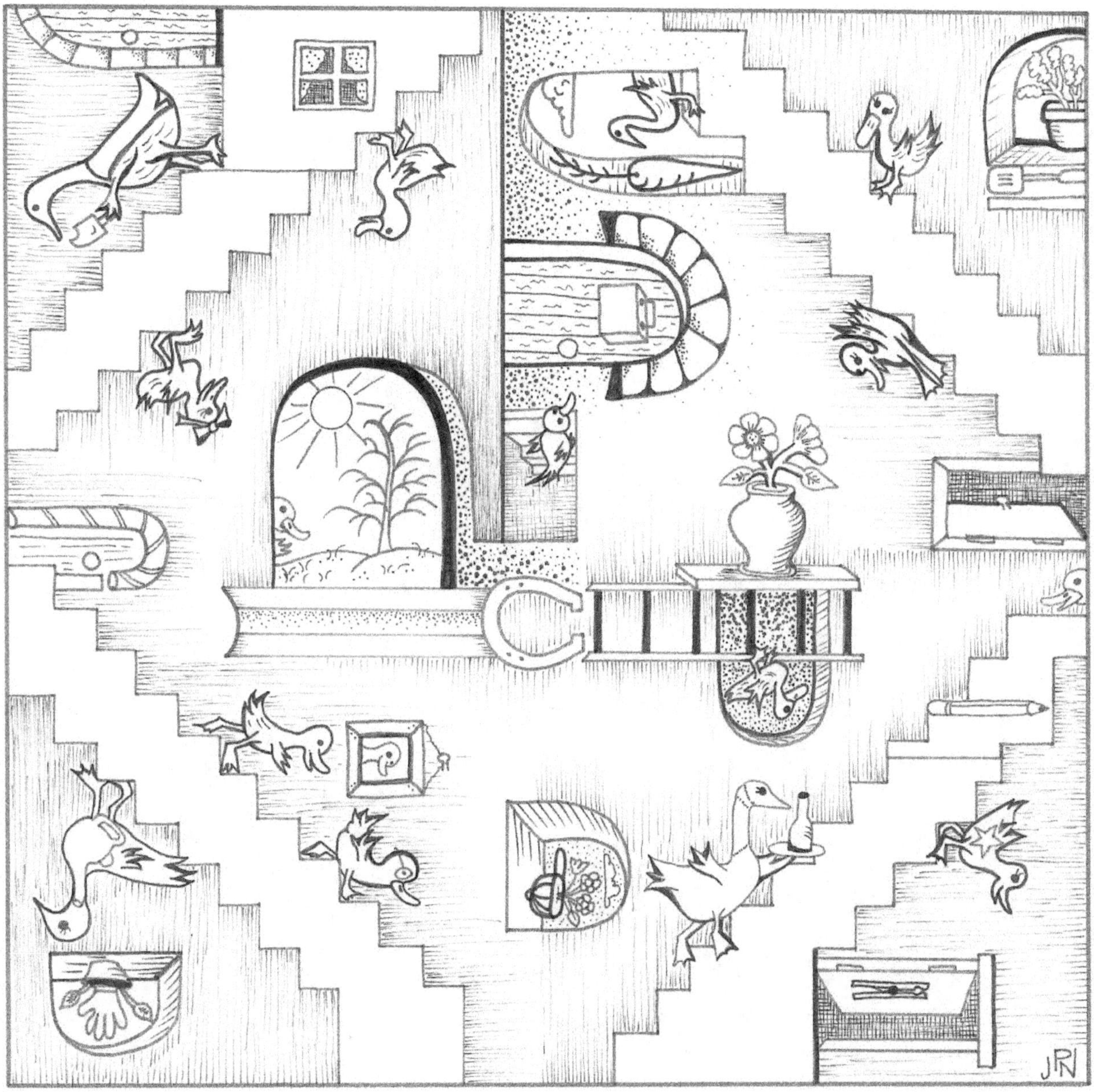

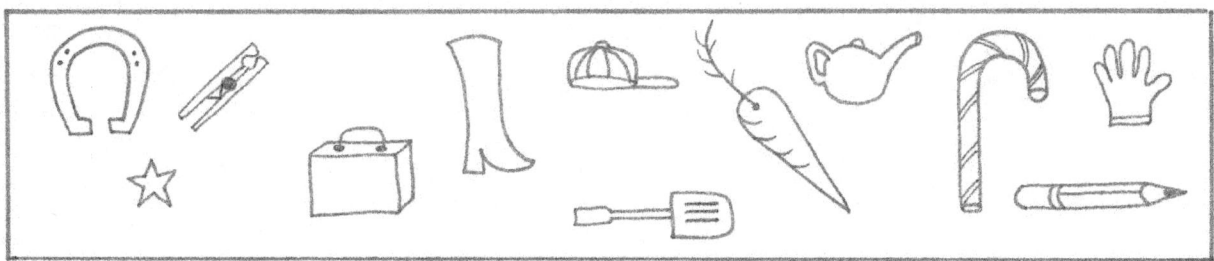

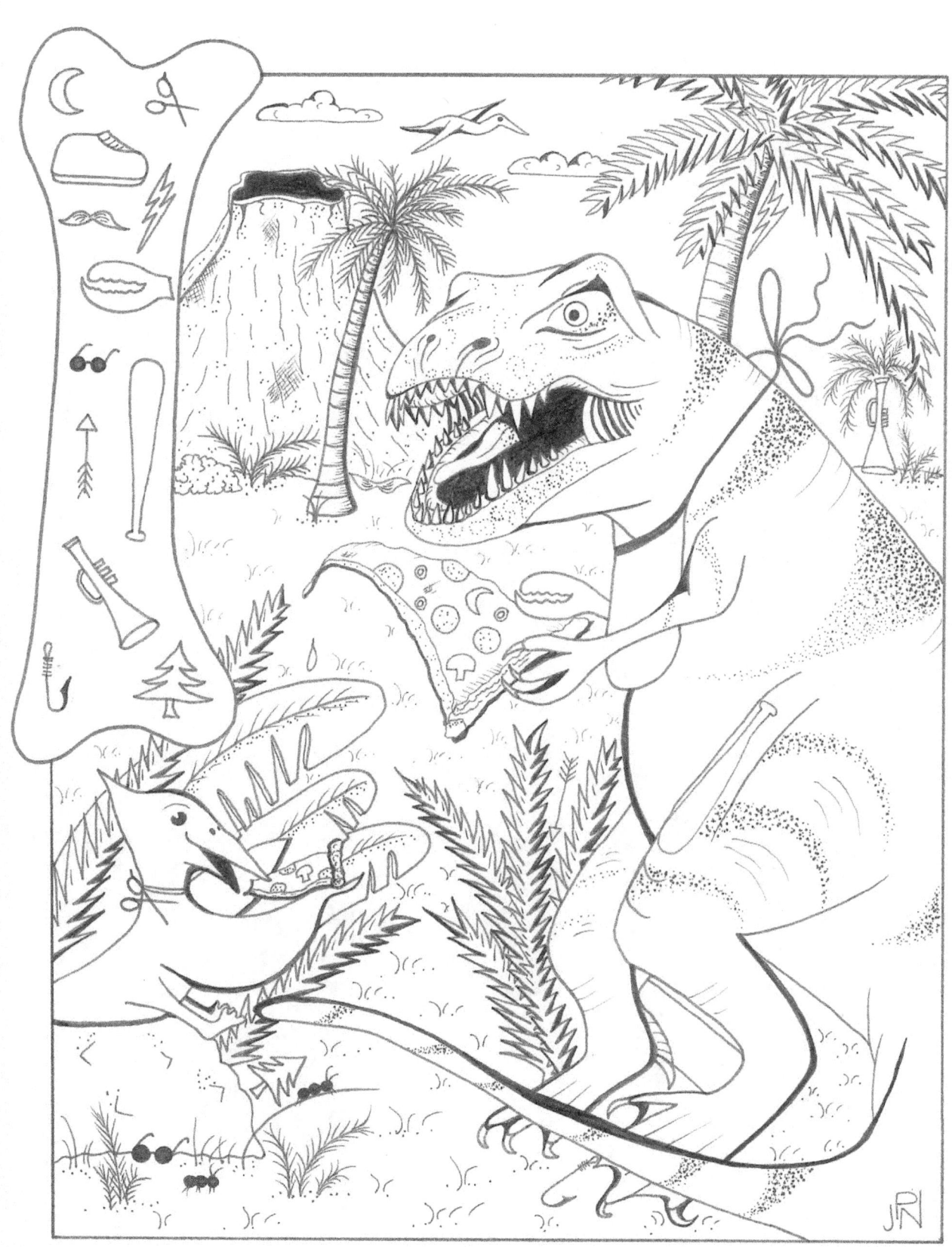

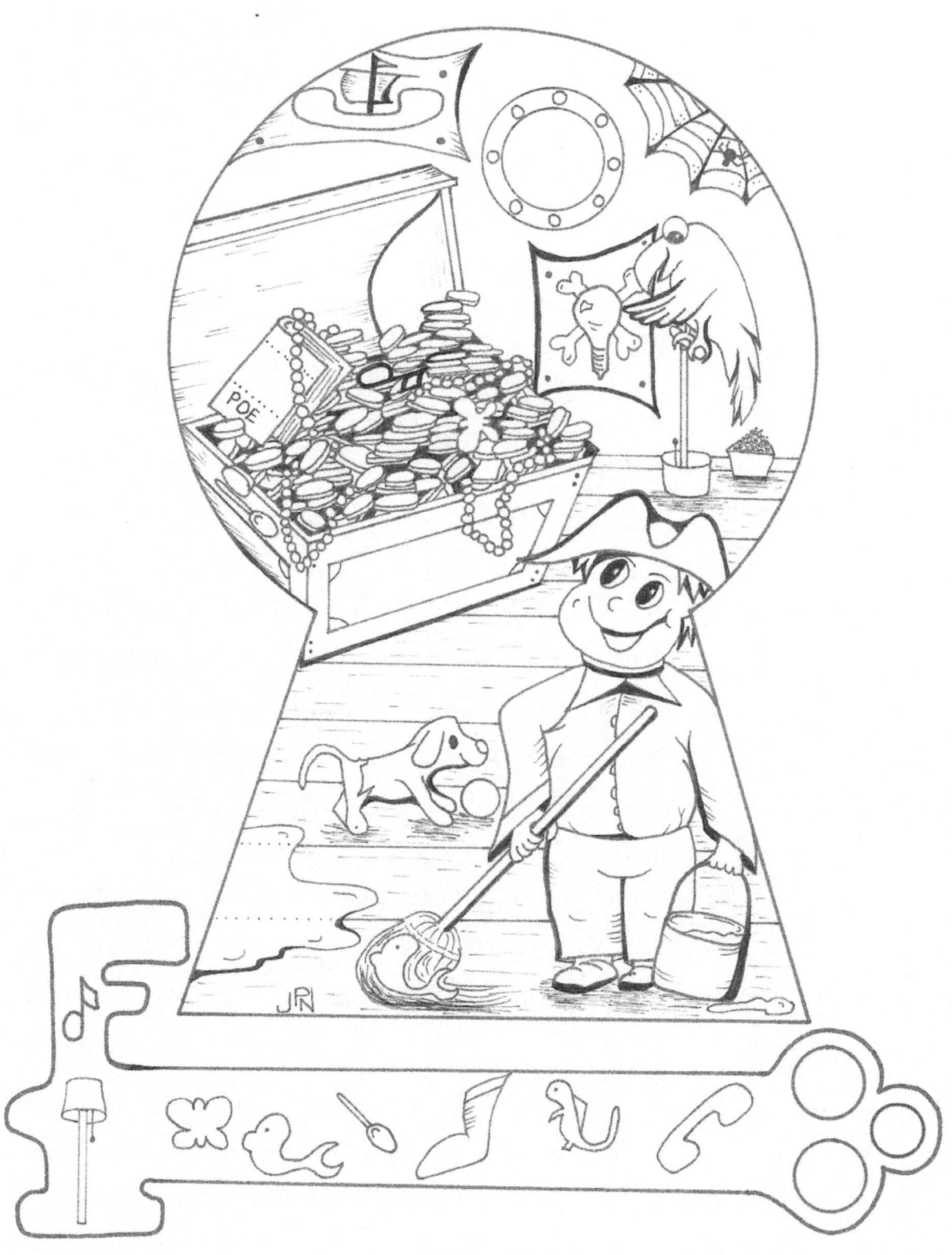

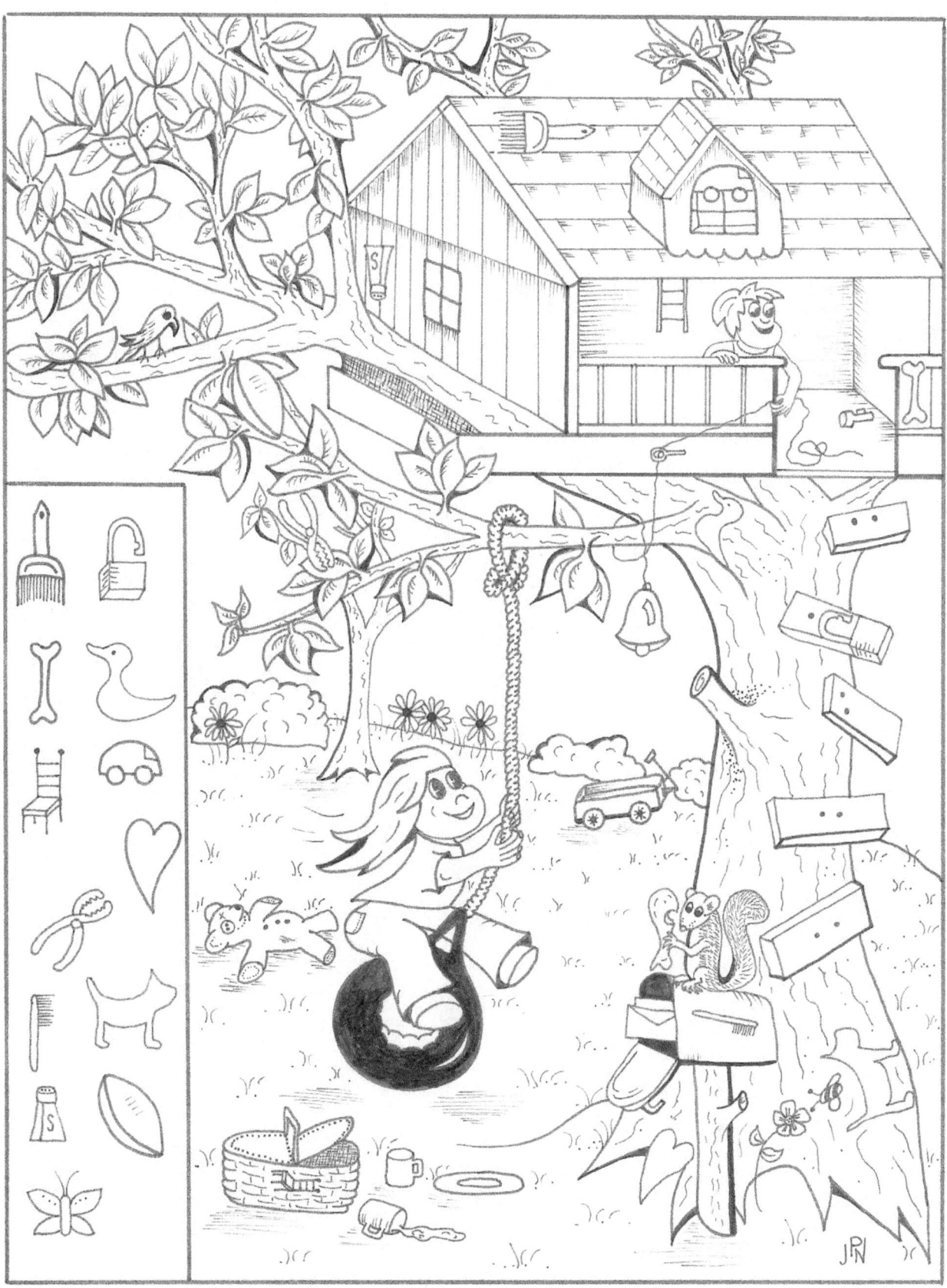

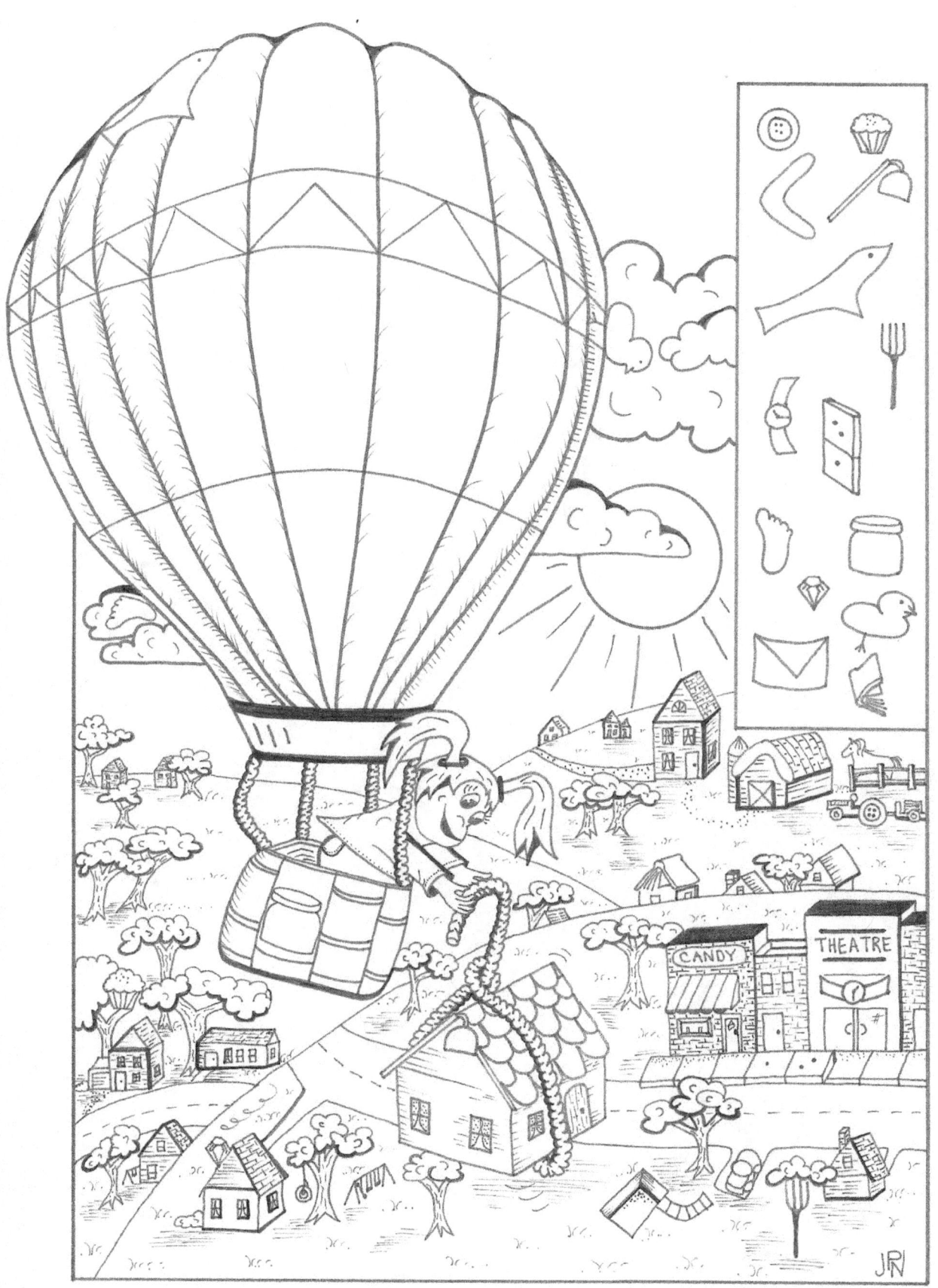

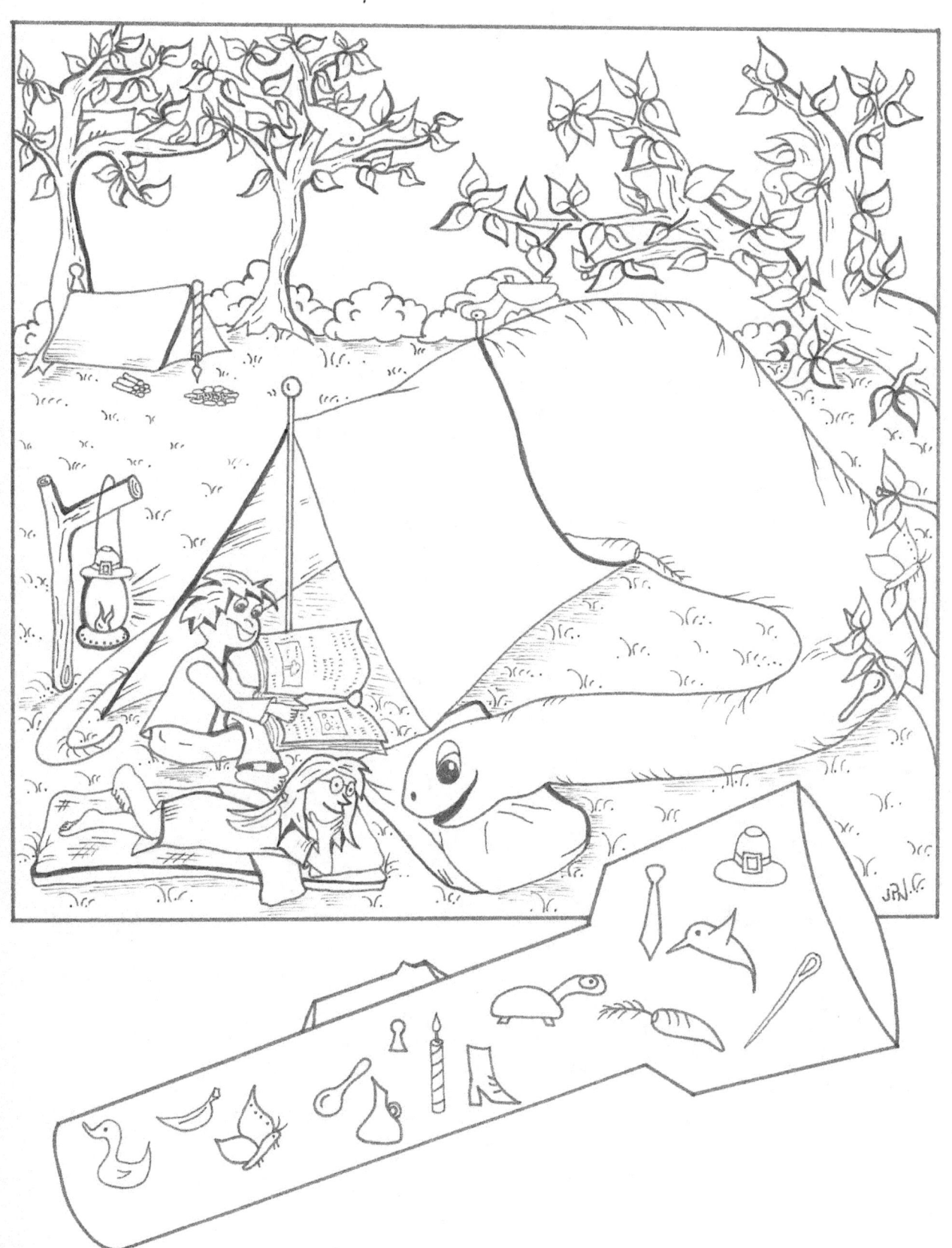

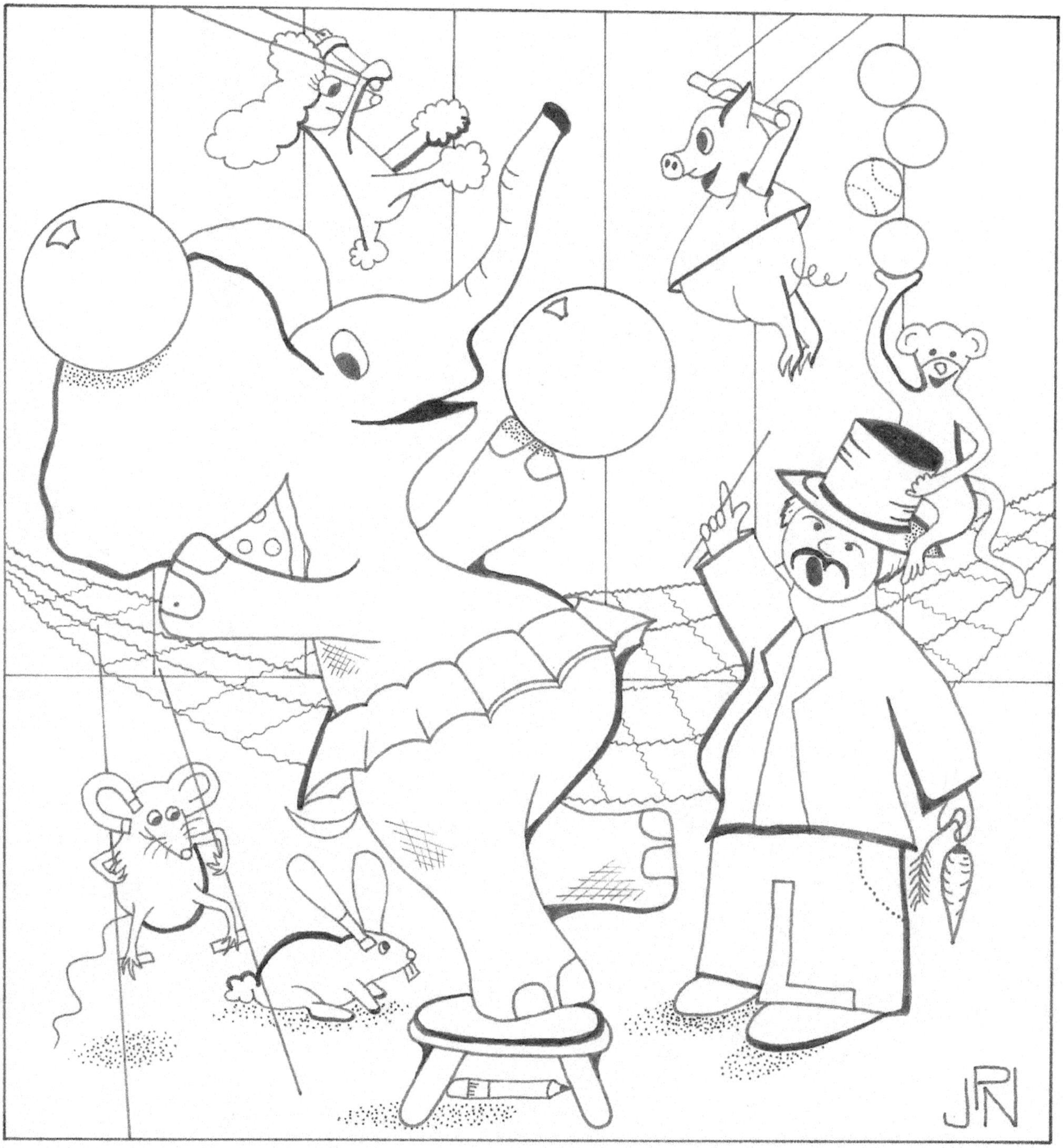

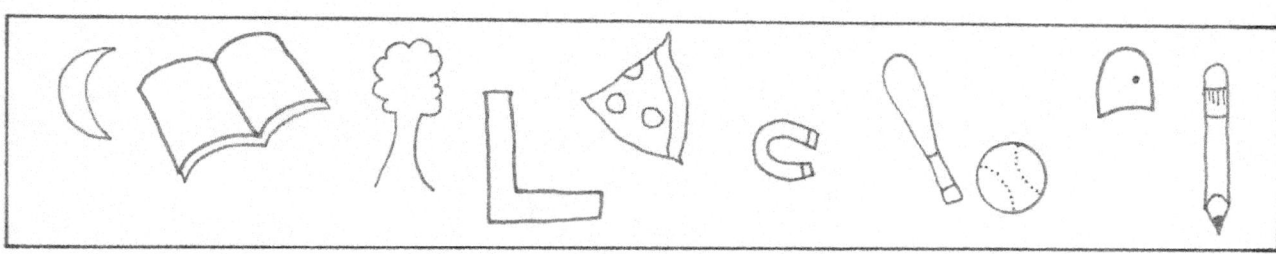

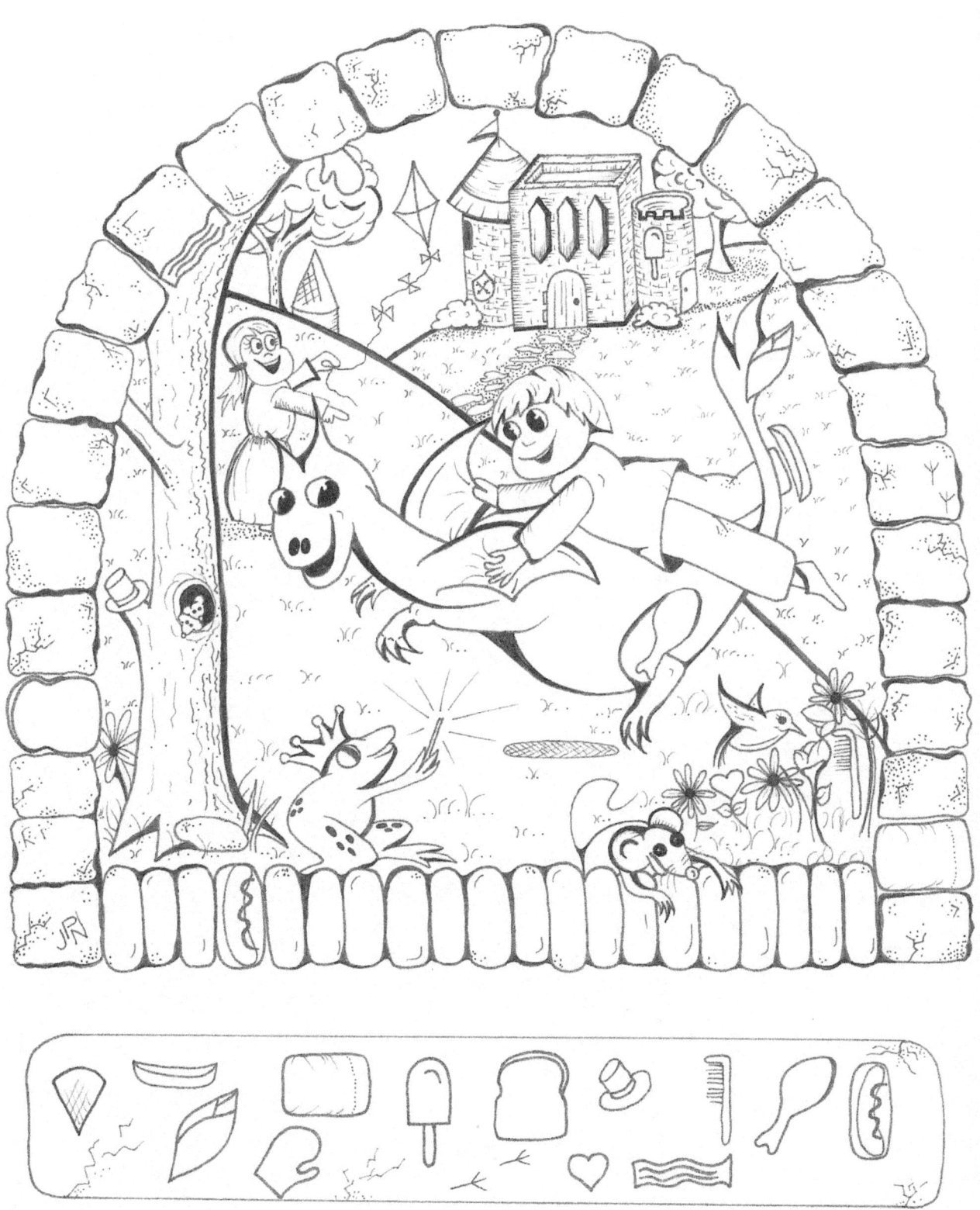

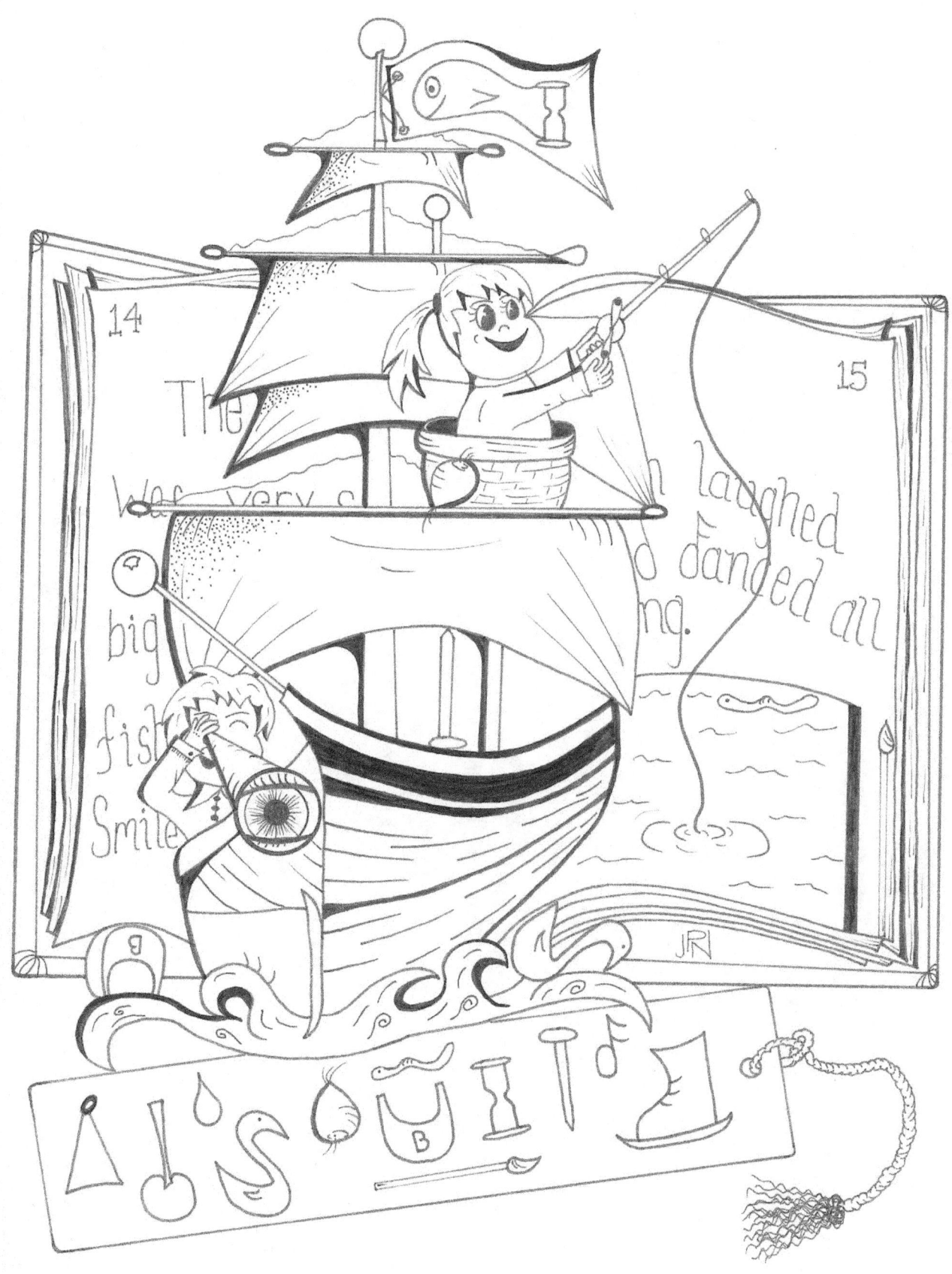

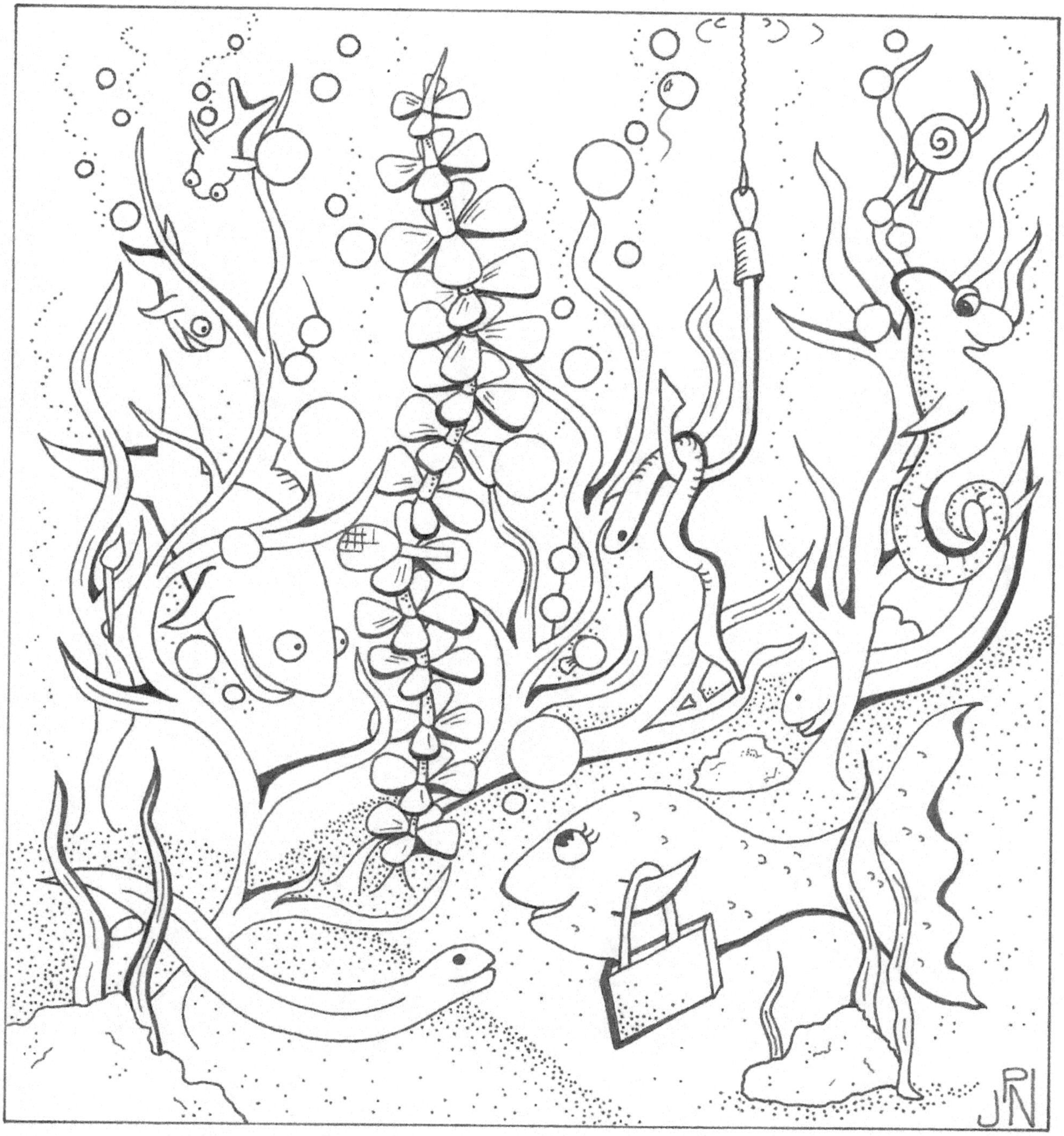

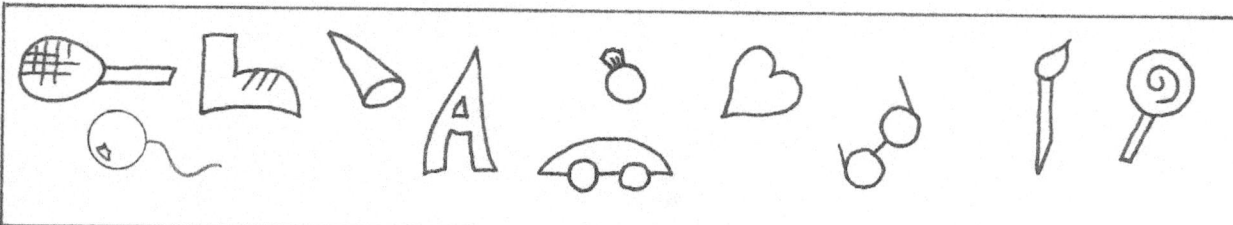

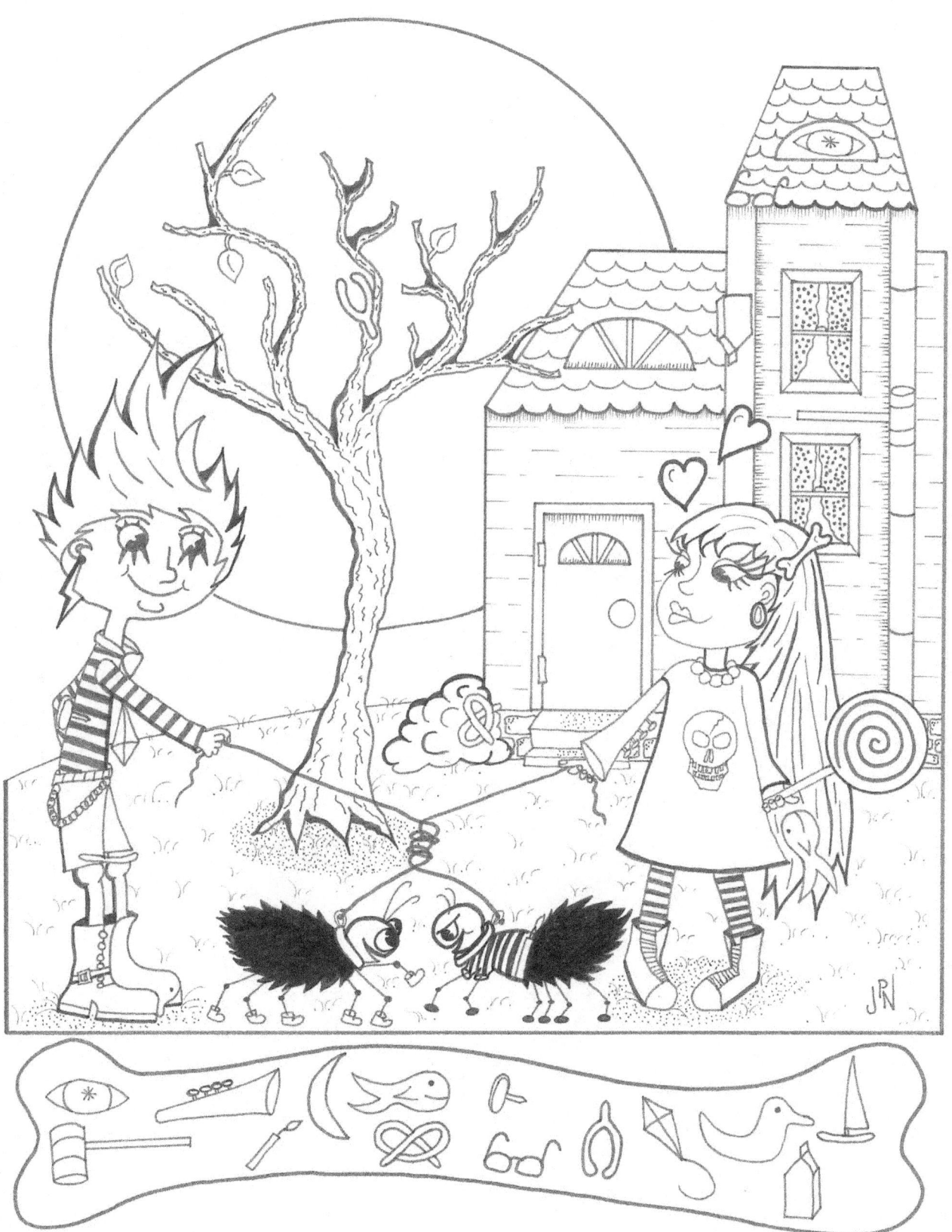

If you're stuck on any of the hidden objects, the answers are highlighted on www.jenniemathisnelson.com, where you will find other fun things and information on upcoming books!


**Also from Jennie Mathis Nelson:**

**My Artful Meditations** – Through bringing the practices of mindful meditation and art therapy together, this book brings centered wellness to the reader and artist as each page has a guided meditation or *thoughts to focus on* as the peaceful image is colored.

Here's a sneak peek from **Artful Meditations**:

Meditation is a quieting of the daily noise that can hijack our thoughts, and this shift in consciousness can allow our true creative inner self to emerge. With practice, we can make a permanent connection with this peaceful and creative side of ourselves.

With each color you add to the pineapple, focus your thoughts on what you add to the world around you and to the people in your life. In a deep and meaningful way, you yourself bring color, life, and abundance to the world and all that you come in contact with. Just as the smallest pebble can have a large and lasting ripple effect, keep your focus on the color you add and feel the joy and peace in that place.

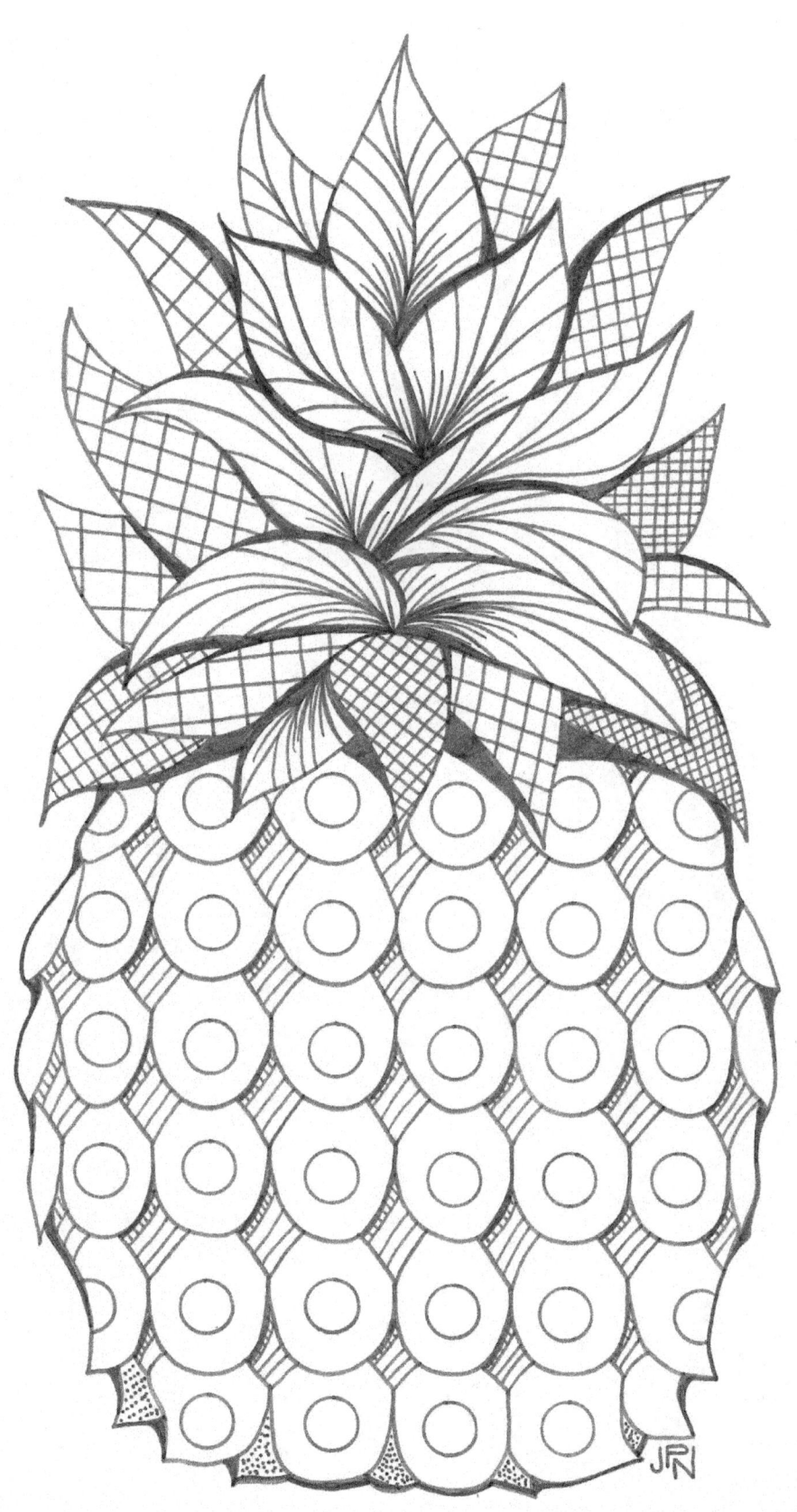

www.ingramcontent.com/pod-product-compliance
Lightning Source LLC
Chambersburg PA
CBHW080621180526
45168CB00007B/3003